Green Gardens of Life

Elizabeth Heij
Green Gardens of Life

Green Gardens of Life
ISBN 978 1 76109 076 9
Copyright © text Elizabeth Heij 2021
Cover: botanical collage by Elizabeth Heij

First published 2021 by
GINNINDERRA PRESS
PO Box 3461 Port Adelaide 5015
www.ginninderrapress.com.au

Contents

Foreword	7
Love, hate, and something more	9
Fire	11
Wandering albatross	13
Strange compulsion	14
Daydreaming	16
On sharing a lover's memories	19
Sorrow	21
A recipe for Gossip	22
Tomorrow's love	24
The iron butterfly	25
I wish I had listened to Grandpa	26
Charlie's big fish	30
Sonnet – Acknowledging the sea	34
Beachcombing at dusk	35
Parting	40
Surprised by delight	41
No tomorrow	43
Bird of solitude	44
North wind in summer	45
Todays	47
Damn You!	48
Sonnet – There was a tree	49
The big trees of Waipoua Kauri Forest	50
The long goodbye	51
Too many hats!	52
Song of life	55
Storms	56
Now, for the first time	57
Lavender	58

Candlelight	59
Love is a flower	61
Little girl – little flower	62
Dawn of womanhood	63
Love letters	64
The sun in your hair	65
You touched my day	68
Perfection at sunset	69
Christmas dinner was scrumptious	70
Woman with flowers	72
The desert wind	73
Reconciling	74
Tears and ecstasy	75
The anchor and the wind	76
A better life	77
Images of love	78
No gift of love	79
The prophets	80
Why?	82
Reconciliation: Returning	83
Te Wai-Iti morning	84
Reflection	86
For a troubled woman friend	87
Sonnet –What chance of eco-harmony?	88
Why does my heart sing?	89
Pain	90
Who are you?	92
The Other Woman	93
There was a man	94
When I was lost	96
After the storm	97
Pity the troubadour	98

Foreword

Much in my work comes from a deep reverence for the natural world, particularly plants in both wild and garden settings, and from the sea in all its infinite moods. This reverence has been there from early childhood, encouraged by a botanist father and artist mother.

I was also encouraged in high school, by a special English teacher, to love and respect the written word; to appreciate the expression of emotion and passion through metaphor; and to have the confidence to describe feelings this way in poetry.

But then a strange thing happened on the way to a career. I trained as a scientist rather than a wordsmith, principally because science offered a more reliable living than writing. The result was creative tension throughout my working life between 'left-brain' science and 'right-brain' metaphor. At times, both suffered!

My personal life has been, as you might say, well lived in. I have been married three times, lived and worked in three different countries, and jointly raised a family of four children. There have been long periods where the clamour of life's daily demands banished creative writing altogether.

There was one period, however, where poetry broke out of its confines in spectacular fashion. Between my first and second marriages, I had two additional loving relationships. One cast me in the proverbial 'mistress' role but, unconventionally, across two counties and an ocean. He was a 'right-brain' person who encouraged me to share my feelings with him at a distance in written poetry. The other relationship was what today might be termed 'friends with benefits'. We knew we were together only so long as the fun lasted, but happy to enjoy what we made of each other's affectionate company for that time.

My third marriage has given me not just love, but peace and the confidence to explore writing again. This time, much of the output is purely for fun. Love, friendship and laughter have been fused into one precious whole. Thank you, Johannes Heij.

Love, hate, and something more

Once, long ago, we were lovers, you and I,
Drawn together by the passionate fire of youth.
Our world was beautiful. A bright future beckoned,
Each new experience intense with shared discovery.

So we took that path; we set our feet upon it.
For a time, it led us through green gardens of delight;
But slowly the colours faded; the way became stony,
And we found ourselves lost in the grey sameness of living.

Eventually, life's drudgery overwhelmed us,
We began to fight our own fights; to follow different paths.
We came to resent the ties that bound us. Full of hate,
We shed them and left love behind us in the bitter dust.

Then, shocked by aloneness, missing remembered illusion,
We sought once more the passion we had lost.
We each found others, who brought new promises,
New pathways, other gardens, and other hopes of love.

As years rolled on, we learned so slowly
The lesson we had failed to understand when young.
The gardens and the wilderness, delight and drudgery,
Sunlight and grey cloud, joy and sorrow, are all one.

So now we come to the final stage of life's long journey,
Both alone at last with nothing left to seek.
A twist of fate has brought us to the same place of care.
I come across you dozing in a garden in the sun.

The sudden shock of recognition stops and stills me.
Our love, our hate, our pain, all flash before my mind;
And then comes a growing warmth of something more than these.
You open your eyes and slowly smile in recognition.

Perhaps, after all, we can finally be friends.

Fire

Fire and Humanity – Humanity and Fire:
We are tied throughout history, from the ancient depths of time,
Master and servant, servant and master, even down to today.

Fire speaks:

I was here before your first human thoughts.
I was a masterful god, a demon spirit,
Riding the lightning bolts that crashed from the sky.
You were helpless before me, fleeing through trees and caves.
Yet I had compassion for your weakness.
I comforted you with light and warmth in the dark and cold
  of the night,
I kept you safe from the terror of teeth and claws.
I coaxed you down from the trees to run fearless over the land,
And became the foundation of your human world.

Humanity speaks:

You became precious to me. I carried you with me.
I cared for you as we walked across the land.
I tamed you, and learned how to bring you forth as a willing
  servant.
Over the ages, I learned a myriad ways for you to serve me,
To light my way, grow and prepare my food, help me across
  the land and waters,
And ever subdue my enemies.
You are my servant, and we have become inseparable.

Fire speaks:

Yes, I am your servant now, but I have not forgotten.
Sometimes I have a wild need to be free, to remind you of our ancient bargain.
Sometimes I yearn to escape, dancing rich red across the landscape,
Feeding greedily on all before me, an image from your ancient nightmares.
I am as I always have been. I may serve you today
But remember I may turn again into your master tomorrow.

Wandering albatross

I am the spirit of flight primeval,
Born to an endless today.
I am the voice of the storm and the waters,
And a child of the white sea spray.

Fill my wings with the winds of the heavens,
And my heart with the light of the sky.
Spread the sea like a carpet below me
And lift me aloft to fly.

Strange compulsion

Dark landscape,
Silver and grey.
The wind sighs over the dunes
Bending the heads of the grasses,
Whispering as it passes,
Carrying hissing sand
Against the sea-washed heaps of driftwood.

Moonlight.
The sea is covered with the fleeting shadows
Of clouds scudding across the face of the moon.
The breakers are driven beneath the wind.
White wavelets run hissing across the grey of the sand.

On my lips
Salt spray stings like a future kiss,
And the wind, passionate, like a future lover
Seeks to lift my clothes away,
And comb its teasing fingers through my hair,

Wild beauty.
This is no night for sleeping.
My heart is too full with a name as yet unknown,
And my thoughts too wakeful for sleep.

Strange compulsion.
The far horizon draws my running feet
Along the silver path to the moon
Reflected trembling in the moving water.

We have yet to meet, you and I,
And I am still unfolding to love,
But I hear your voice in the wind.
I see your face in the shadows,
And your eyes in the changing light on the sea.

Daydreaming

Let's leave this existence
For just a few hours
To walk in the meadow
And smile at the flowers.
We can sit by the tree
And look up to the snows
And the breeze will be gentle
And cool as it blows
Through the branches above us
High in the tree
With a whispering sound
Like the far distant sea,
And blossoms will fall
Like rain in the spring
In our laps, on our hair,
And with joy we will sing
Of the days and the nights
Of the love we will share
And the warmth in our hearts
That will always be there,
And our lips will be cool
In that high mountain air,
But the fire of your kisses
Will set me aflame.

I'll come to you, cling to you,
Whisper your name –
Oh take me and love me.
My love is for you,
As high as the mountains,
As deep as the blue
Of the sky far above us,
As sweet as a flower.
Please fill all my longing,
Please give me this hour
Of your loving, your giving,
Your warmth and your touch.
I need you, my lover.
I want you so much.
And then if you love me
With the blossoms above,
My eyes will be bright
With the tears of my love,
And our hour will have passed
Like the snowdrops in spring,
But because of the snowdrops
My heart will still sing
With the song of the joy
Of the gift of your love,
Like flowers in the mountains

With the warm sun above.
The blossoms may fall
From the branches each spring
But again they return
And my heart will still sing.
Each springtime the snowdrops
May last but a while,
But they always return –
And forever I'll smile.

On sharing a lover's memories

That day you shared with me your childhood home,
Its rooms still echoing with memories of the past,
I saw with happiness the joy you'd known
Before the boy became a man at last.

I saw you run beside a loving father,
Your face alert with smiles and boyish pride,
The man, the boy, each company for the other,
The tall tree with the sapling by its side.

I saw the youth. He touched me with his shyness.
I went with him to that first high-school ball.
Here is the door through which he went to college,
The door through which he heard his future call.

And then the rest of life before you,
A forking highway turning left or right,
One fork a life within the world that knew you,
The other stretching far, obscured from sight.

Now comes a room you may not wish to show me.
I will not chide you if you close the door.
Your house has many riches that I can see.
I will not ask for you to show me more.

And now I feel a darkness filled with sorrow.
Your pain is like the winter's icy cold.
The tree has fallen, and you step into tomorrow,
Carrying with pride the name you hold.

And still it turns – the wheel keeps turning.
You are the tall tree now. Your seed is sown.
Your daughter runs beside you, learning,
Your pride her future and your love her home.

So what will I be in your house of memories, Lover?
The wind that sighs in winter round the eaves,
The breeze that stirs your hair on springtime mornings
And whispers in the piles of autumn leaves?

Sorrow

Sorrow is a friend who comes to find us,
To touch us gently but with winter's chill.
Sorrow's eyes are red with weeping,
The laughter silent and the dancing still.

And in the silence sorrow holds us,
Sorrow and love beside us, hand in hand,
And dimly seen those other feelings scatter
Like seabirds flying towards a distant land.

Gently, with love, sorrow will guide us
To where they have vanished from our sight,
And we will find peace to walk with sorrow,
And step once more with laughter into light.

A recipe for Gossip

There's nothing like a saucy tale to prime the gossip pot
Just stir it well, add lots of spice, and serve it piping hot.
Such a tale was started by the wife of Sheriff Brewster
She was seen one night with a mystery man, an oily-looking rooster!

Down the alley, behind the bank, they slid with backward glances
But the watcher didn't follow on. She didn't like her chances.
What were these two doing in the misty moon's pale light
Heading for the bayou on a hot and humid night?

Well, you should have heard the gossip that travelled like the breeze.
There was kinky sex, a big bank heist, or maybe both of these.
Deputy Iles thought, at last, he'd better warn his boss
So hat-in-hand he told him of the hot and spicy goss.

Sheriff Brewster, pompous fool, did not believe the tale
His belly shook with laughter and he wheezed like an autumn gale
His 'little woman'? Don't be silly – no interest in sex at all
And too little wit to cope with any more than a shopping mall!

He thought, however, they'd better check the 'oily-rooster' guy
So Iles went off to question all the people standing by.
Like a 'library' of novels his notebook soon became
As everyone gave a different tale and a different possible name

So many naughty stories! But he stupidly landed in strife
By failing to question Deputy Tanker and the Sheriff's lovely wife
Now, William Tanker, a handsome man and favourite with the ladies
Was much too smooth and slippery to get tied up by queries

And Lou-Anne Brewster, wide-eyed, innocent, inestimable lady
Was patently incapable of doing something 'shady'
So still he searches while the Sheriff laughs, and the gossip goes around
And the pair who fired the gossip up, have a tasty love nest found.

So is 'oil' the magic ingredient used by William Tanker?
Or is he just a philandering SOB of a…
…fine Deputy Sheriff of the great State of 'Loosiana', USA.

Tomorrow's love

Young lovers,
I see you strolling in the park,
Arms around each other,
Your eyes on each other's faces,
And laughter in your voices.

You are full of today,
But I have both yesterday and tomorrow.
You feel the breath of your springtime,
But I feel the full glow of my summer.

You step lightly in your love,
But mine is a pair of wings with which to fly.
Your love is like the morning's early light,
But mine is like the rainbow –
A spectrum of feelings,
Richer than you have ever known.

Perhaps you will not understand
Until your today becomes tomorrow.
Perhaps you do not even see me
Walking alone.

The iron butterfly

You found me among the green leaves of my youth,
Pretending to be bold,
Showing only my false face,
So young, believing I was old.
In love, you tried to hold me,
To make me belong.
In my own self-doubt I followed,
Not knowing right from wrong,
Never wholly yielding,
Never wholly free,
A prisoner of illusions
Of what life ought to be,
Illusions of identity, lasting until
With a cry of bitterness and a silken skein,
My dreams no longer fitting,
I wove my cocoon of pain.
Inward seeking,
No answer could I find;
Inward thrusting
To burst the bubble in my mind.
And now the cocoon is breaking.
Pain, love, loneliness and living are one.
I am emerging.
My wings are drying in the sun.
I am an iron butterfly
With a heart of stone.
I must face my new life,
And I must fly alone.

I wish I had listened to Grandpa

I wish I had listened to Grandpa
As he sat by the fire in his chair:
'You must never go up
To the attic, young pup.
There's a monster will get you up there!'

I thought I had heard that old monster
Bumbling around overhead
Puffing and shunting
And scuffling and grunting
Above me while I was in bed

Well, mostly I listened to grown-ups
And mostly I did as they said,
But boys will be boys
And, bored with my toys
I decided to go look instead.

Come on Billy, I said to my brother
Let's peek in the attic and see
If a monster is there
Or it's just Grandpa's scare
To keep us both close to his knee

So quietly while Grandpa was dozing
Up we crept to the very top landing
We looked up at the hatch
But our height was no match
We couldn't get there by just standing

I know, I said then to Billy
We can stack up my desk, shelf and chair
You hold them tightly
And I'll climb up lightly
We'll soon find out just what's up there

Quietly we piled up a big stack of stuff
And slowly I started to climb
I got up to the top
It was quite a big drop
But I didn't think much at the time

I reached up my arms to the ceiling
Though I had to let go of the chair
I undid the latch
And opened the hatch
And lifted it slowly with care

I couldn't see anything up there
It was dark and as black as can be
'Billy, go get the torch
Grandpa keeps in the porch
Without it there's nothing to see'

Billy came back double quick with the torch
And carefully passed it to me
I pointed the beam
And let out a scream
At the two eyes that looked back at me

Oh help! It's the monster. I see him
What a terrible, horrible fright
I let go of the stack
And fell hard on my back
Then everything went black as night

When I woke up I saw Grandpa
With a thunderous frown on his face
You stupid young pup
You have really messed up
Look what you've done to the place

The chair and the torch were both broken
And my arm was hurting so much
My ankle as well
Felt like absolute hell
Was I going to need a crutch?

Grandpa carried me down to the clinic
Where they gave me a pain-killing pill
The nurse was a dragon
She kept on and on naggin'
At me to keep everything still

Now I'm laid up in bed with plaster
All around my arm and my leg
I'm so bored I could shout
But I'm not allowed out
No matter how much I beg

Once Grandpa got over his anger
He laughed at me time after time
And he was sorry for Blossom
Our resident possum
Whose fright was much greater than mine

So –
If you want to go up to your attic
Don't do what I tried to do
Listen carefully to me
I'm now wise as can be
Use a ladder and head torch too.

Charlie's big fish

Grandpa, can you take us fishing?
I asked one spring morning so fine
Let's go down to the lake
And catch fish to bake
We've got our new rods, hooks, and line.

So Billy and I went with Grandpa
Walking down to the lake for some fun
We tied on our bait
And sat down to wait
While Grandpa dozed off in the sun.

The air was soft, warm and drowsy
Scented by flowers in the grass
Little birds twittered
And dragonflies flitted
With a soft buzzing sound as they passed.

Billy got drowsy like Grandpa
And went off to sleep on his back
But I kept on fishing
I really was wishing
For a big fish to put in my sack

At last came a swish in the water
It was something fast, speckled with black
My rod gave a jiggle
The line gave a wriggle
But then the whole thing went slack.

Carefully I looked in the water
But the worm was gone from my hook
Some thieving old trout
Had sussed my line out
And stolen the bait – what a crook!

That made me determined to catch him
I tied on a new wriggly worm
I cast out the line
That fish would be mine!
I sat down and held the rod firm

Pretty soon he was back for a second quick snack
Sneaking out with a swish and a splash
He grabbed at the bait
But he sure didn't wait
He swam off with it quick as a flash

That made me so mad. I felt I'd been had!
How dare he do that to me!
I tied bait on once more
Dropped the line near the shore
And stayed close to the edge so I'd see

Soon he came out, that sneaky old trout
He was getting too daring and rash
But this time I was ready
I held the rod steady
Then leapt in on top with a splash

I grabbed him up tight with all of my might
And held on whilst kicking to float
He flapped and he flailed
But I now had his scales
Stuck tight in the wool of my coat

Grandpa! I shouted. Please come and help.
I've caught an enormous great trout!
Grandpa leapt up to see
What had happened to me
And he reached down to help pull me out.

Once out on the bank, standing dripping and wet
I let go of the fish with a flop
Then in a trice
Though it wasn't so nice
Grandpa fixed him for good with a rock

Billy was very impressed with my catch
Come on, Charlie, let's go and show Dad.
I was shivering with cold
Now, not quite so bold
And my wet clothes they smelled pretty bad

Look, Billy yelled to Mum in the kitchen
Charlie has caught a huge trout
I held it up proudly
But Mum just said loudly
Off you go to the laundry. Get out!

You're covered with slime, fish scales and grime
And I think you have ruined your coat.
I wish you two boys
Could just play with your toys
Or catch fish from a nice clean boat.

Then she turned round to our grandpa
And gave him a scolding severe
You silly old fool
To let them fall in the pool
You should have kept them well clear!

Mum's bark is always much worse than her bite
She got over it all like she ought.
And she sure thought my trout
Was the best fish out
Though she laughed at the way it was caught.

(And we all thought it tasted pretty good too!)

Sonnet – Acknowledging the sea

For the widow of a yachtsman

I hold you close and look across the bay,
The troubled water green and streaked with white,
The sky above me filled with clouds of grey,
The day now fading fast to misty night.

I saw you first so many years ago
Standing tall and bronzed there on the sand,
Looking out to sea to check the flow
Of weather that a sailor might command.

The sea and I we ever shared your love;
Embraces warm cocooned in sun-drenched dunes,
The thrill of mastering the waves and wind above;
In later years quiet beachside afternoons.

Your ashes now I scatter. As my loving last goodbye
A lone red rose kissed and tossed up to the misty sky.

Beachcombing at dusk

Under the pure deep blue of the crimson-bordered sky
The gulls fly so high that their cry
Is forever lost in the great emptiness.
The last rays of the setting sun pick out their wheeling white
  bodies
In red and gold against the blue.

'Where are you?'
'I am here by your side. Come.
Together let us follow the tide down across the sand.'
'Teach me to understand the secrets of the sea.'
'Follow me. I will show you treasures which the tide leaves
  behind –
The ones many find but few understand.'

The waves are gentle tonight. The fading light
Gleams white on their smooth crests.
With a slow sinuous motion they rise from the level waters
  behind them,
Monsters of molten green glass, but oh so cool and gentle.
Then as they near the land, slowly they bend and fall with a
  sigh,
Spread hissing across the sand and die at their journey's end.

'What have the waves carried to my feet,
Wrapped in foam and tied with strands of green weed?'
'This is treasure indeed!
Feel the cold smoothness inside the shell.
Look – On the outside is written an old Arabic spell.
The symbols are faint and worn, but the mystery lingers.
Trace the soft curves of the markings with your fingers.
Listen. The voice of the great Sea Mother comes from the
    darkness within.'

'Tell me, what is she saying?'
'You are a child of the Sea. The Sea is your mother.
You understand one another.' 'What else does she say?'
'Ah, she is calling us away! Come.'

Beneath my feet the waves no longer sigh.
The sand beneath my feet is dry.
I can no longer walk, although I try.
With every step my feet sink deeper through the cool silken
    surface
Into the sun's warmth still trapped beneath.
My limbs are weighed with lead.
'Oh let us not walk! Instead let us lie here.'

I fill my hand but cannot hold the sand.
Minute fragments of ages past,
Cast by the waters in astronomical drifts,
Each is an infinitesimal world of its own –
Timeless and ageless, each with its own form and colour.
Oh, infinite variety! Oh, limitless beauty!
See how the slightest breath disturbs a million worlds.

'What have I found beneath the sand?
What is this shape and what does it mean?'
'This is a fragment of some landlocked giant
That grew perhaps on a mountain, its roots deep in snow.'
'How the mighty are brought low!' 'But no!
There is beauty in this tortured form.
The boughs of this tree were twisted by the wind,
And knotted in the struggle with the storm.'
'The wood is so white, rimed with a frosting of crystalline salt.'
'The waves have worn away one shape
And a thousand more are born,
Phantom children of the ocean
Which exist in the mind and are never shared.
But, to you, my thoughts are bared,
For you are also of the mind.'
'We are of the sea-kind. We are both the same.'
'It is inevitable. All life returns to the sea from whence it came.'
'Let us go back to the sea.'

The chill of the water strikes the body
Like a thrill of mingled pleasure and pain.
The night is like black velvet,
But the surface of the water is a lake of green fire.
'What is this that glows with inner light?'
'This is the green grass of the sea,
The living glow of tiny creatures you cannot see.'
Each movement is illuminated and lives beyond its duration;
Each ripple is outlined in its motion.

The sea is gentle tonight.
The sand is soft beneath my feet.
The waves touch my body like a thousand tiny stroking hands.
My heart's beat rises and falls with the swell.
So this is the ultimate secret of my Sea Mother.
At last we understand one another.
I am one with the water.
I have melted and dissolved.
I am no longer of the land,
But the ocean's own daughter.
Now I understand.

'Where are you?
There is no longer any light.
I am alone in the dark.
Come back! I'm so afraid.'
We can never understand the sea.
The illusion of knowledge casts us into deeper ignorance,
An abyss so dark – there is no light,
A plight without rescue – there is no aid.
Wait! There is still the Arabic spell.
Here in my hand I still hold the shell.
'Let me hear your voice, Sea Mother.
I am lost and the night is so black.'
Silence! – Despair!
'Come back! Oh, please come back.'

Parting

Each day, the sun rises – golden
Each morning, a clear new start
And it is the same sun that shines for you,
And rises also in my heart.

Each day, the world sings for us –
Your song, my song – sometimes they will blend;
Each day, a new and lovely melody
That, remembered, need never reach an end.

Each day, you are a part of me
And I a part of you. I am a tree
Shaped by the passing touch of you – the wind.
We have known each other and joined, and yet go free,
And even in our silences and our forgetting,
You are a warmth in my heart and the sweet wine of life for me.

Surprised by delight

How can I tell you this feeling inside?
It is so new. Does it even have a name?
You smiled at me,
And your eyes were like a window opened wide,
Beckoning.
Then you touched me,
And nothing could ever be the same.
I had known love – known its laughter and then its pain,
But no one had touched me in that way before –
A caress like the touch of a gentle summer wind,
A touch like the waves of a midnight pier seeking the shore,
A kiss like the leap in my heart on a fairground ride,
Carrying us up among the stars and city lights;
And the closeness of you,
Filling me like the music of a riverboat,
Or the lights of lanterns glowing in the trees.
You were all of the crowd for me. You filled my senses.
And you have given me more, much more than laughter,
More than happiness: new peace, and new defences,
Serenity in the beauty of today,
And a shield against the uncertainty and pain.
When I was incomplete and empty,
You filled me and made me whole again.
And this joy will stay with me when I leave and go away.
Your arms are warm and gentle, and your voice,
In desire speaking softly like the night breeze,
Calls my heart in from the cold of loneliness,
And fills it with the warmth of knowing happiness.
I feel the golden sunlight of a new morning –

A new morning of radiance, deep in my heart.
I come to your arms in peace, in deep delight, and so at ease
It seems as though I live a lifetime with you in one night.
Are you a stranger – or have we loved before?
To know you is to know the warmth of deepest joy.
I am surprised by sweet delight.

No tomorrow

Be careful, dear friend, you say to me
Lest you become for me the things you should not be.
And I smile and touch you, and I say I know
That the seeds of love, though planted, must not grow.
But how to I keep them buried, hidden from the light,
When they have already grown for me and flowered in our delight?
And how can I make you other than who you are to me,
When deep in my heart you are already the man that only you can be.
We have no tomorrow, you and I. Just for today we can belong;
Yet I walk with perfect peace and love, in your house which cannot be my home.
When we come together it seems truly that time is stilled,
For I am lost in a golden warmth of happiness; my emptiness is filled.
You are as real to me as any part of life,
And I am tied to you, deep in my heart, though I am not your wife.

Bird of solitude

Fly little swallow, bird of the springtime,
Into the golden light of the morning sun.
My heart lifts like the wings of the dawn.
I too am the swallow. The earth is below me,
Hidden in shadow and lingering night.

Who follows me?
Only my shadow.
When I fly, my shadow follows always.
When I sing with love my shadow listens in silence.
I climb with joy into the warmth of the sun,
My heart is filled with the bright diamonds of ecstasy.
And though I am solitary, my shadow never leaves me.
I am solitary, but I am never alone.

North wind in summer

You are like the north wind in summer,
That touches all the flowers and passes by.
I am hot, wakeful and restless.
My thoughts of you, like embers,
Are filled with a fire that the north wind
Fans into leaping flames.

Who loves the north wind,
That hot caress that tosses my dreams at night?
You know me everywhere.
I have no secret places.
You share my body, my laughter and my light.

Who loves the touch of your hands,
Like a shiver of sheer delight,
That hot-cold pleasure?
Hold me, my lover. Oh hold me now.
Take my flower of love and blow away the petals.
Let me be your willow. Touch me.
Bend me and let me ride your storm.

Who loves the warmth of your kisses;
Kisses that make me tremble with desire.
Was I born for your kisses? Who knows.
Not even the wind can say.
Is the greatest gift to my body the touch of your mouth?
I know not. But sometimes it truly feels that way.

I love the north wind, my restless lover;
I love you as I find you – strong and warm,
The calm and the storm, but wicked, wild and free.
Where have you come from, my love?
Across the desert.
And where will you sleep tonight?
Out on the restless sea.

Sometimes you take my heart with you, unknowing,
My love, my soul, and the secrets of my mind.
And sometimes I give them to you freely –
Trusting even in the wind.

Todays

I come to you in friendship,
One free spirit to another,
Out of bondage,
With no promises,
No chains,
Ever.

I cannot pledge you all my love.
I will never ask you to give yours.
Love is not ours to promise.
It goes where it wills.
We can only follow
Or suffer.

If in our freedom we find peace
To share a rich measure of friendship
And not feel tied,
Then I will give you 'Todays' without fear,
And we can forget
The 'Forevers'.

Damn You!

Oh damn you, damn you!
Take your lust away
And touch me not
To cause my sister pain.
Her smile is more to me than all your kisses.
What price her happiness – her trust?
You seek in vain
For love in midnight corners, stolen,
Drunken, besotted, shamed
And fumbling in the night.
What will you feel tomorrow, waking?
Pride? Oh damn you!
What do you know of love and feeling?
Love. Love? You mock me.
The word is poisonous on your tongue.
This is not love – or even friendship.
This is not truth or tenderness, or right.
I care more for my sister –
Her pain and tears,
More for her joy and laughter
Than for all the empty words you utter.
Damn you!
Take your lust back to the gutter.
You are not worthy to dry her tears of pain.
You care only for a moment's pleasure.
Love has your measure. Oh God, how vain!
You tread on trust and tenderness,
Break them and leave them lying in the dust,
And wound the one who truly loves you.
Oh damn your lust!

Sonnet – There was a tree

There was a tree that stood atop a hill,
Its shady branches widely spread and green,
Five hundred years from seed, it stood there still,
A forest secret, proud but never seen

There came a traveller from across the seas
Who gazed upon it as it swept the sky.
He saw its sturdy strength defy the breeze,
Imagining a sailor's spar raised high.

The sound of axe and deadly final fall,
The shocking silence of the grieving glade,
With shouts and whips and trampling bullock bawl
The tree into a clipper's mast was made.

But Nature always wins the final fight:
The ship went down, all hands, one stormy night.

The big trees of Waipoua Kauri Forest

Oh Tane Mahuta, Lord of the Forest,
How long have you stood here growing in might?
When Rangi and Papa were locked in embracing
You were but a seedling seeking the light.
Still you cling tightly to Papa the mother,
Your arms reaching up to your father the sky,
And the seasons and storms and the winds they have touched you,
And bent you and shaped you as ages passed by.

Te Matua Ngahere, Father of Forests,
Proudly you stand like a pillar of grey.
The weight of the heavens has lain on your shoulders,
And yet you have stood here through time till today.
The children of Tane have grown in your shadow,
Lifting their arms to the warmth and the light,
And you have been shelter through all of the ages,
For songs of the morning and shapes of the night.

Oh Tane, Matua, majestic, eternal,
We live for an instant and then we are gone,
And when we have passed from this land and this forest,
Still you will stand in the future – alone.

The long goodbye

It has been such a long goodbye, my love,
With the fabric of your being thinning like old linen
Washed to transparency in the river of life

You and I, such a love we shared together,
Joy flowing through us as the wheel of life
Turned through the magic of our days

We had sunshine, rain, and carefree promises
Nights wrapped in the warmth of love
Bright with the prospect of endless tomorrows

But darkness stole upon us all too soon,
And the wheel turned from sunlight into shadow
Stealing our promises and all our tomorrows

When I awoke that morning and you were gone,
The echo of your presence was the whispering of flags in the wind
Giving me love and strength to send you on that final journey

Your echo lives forever in my soul, beloved,
And in the shining child we created together,
Born of love like a prayer that spreads its beauty in the world
   forever

Too many hats!

A cautionary tale for grown-ups: beware of trying to wear too many hats!

I love hats. They're so pretty. They cheer up my day.
'How pretty you look!' is what people say.

When I'm wearing my hats, I feel happy and glad,
Hats are the best things that I've ever had.

I have hats in the wardrobe and under the bed;
And as many as possible up on my head.

I have big ones and little ones – red, green, and blue;
Pink, black and purple – and yellow ones too.

They have flowers on, and bells on, and feathers so tickly;
And little lace pieces all stiff, white and prickly.

I get more hats as presents; buy hats from the shop,
Each one of them just right to go up on top.

How could I ever put on only one?
More and more hats give me more and more fun.

I love people saying, 'How marvellous you are.'
'How lovely!' 'How pretty!' and 'Oh what a star!'

More and more hats – well, isn't this grand.
Suddenly, though, I feel too tired to stand.

Oh dear, I feel sick; and what's wrong with my knees
They almost fold up every time that I sneeze.
And my feet are so sore – they hurt like a bruise
Perhaps what I need is a new pair of shoes.

Sandals are good. My toes can hang out.
Surely this helps what the pain is about.
My feet are in trouble there's no doubt of that.
So I'll cheer myself up with a lovely new hat.

But now I feel worse and more tired than ever.
I'd best see the doctor. He's very clever.

Oh Doctor Proctor, do help me please,
I have terrible pains in my poor feet and knees.
I'm dreadfully tired. I can't leave my bed.
It's all I can do to keep hats on my head.

Doctor Proctor said, 'Hmmmm! Now what have we here?
Do you have any pain in your head or your ear?

It's a case of *Hatitis* that's getting you down.
You must take all the hats off and really lie down.
Though each of these hats is light as a feather,
How heavy they are when you wear them together!'

But doctor, I scared to take off my hats,
I'm frightened that people will think I've gone bats!

'I'm sorry, they have to come off now, today.
(And here is my bill. You have two weeks to pay.)'

So I took off my hats and lay down to sleep.
It felt so fantastic, I stayed there a week.

And when I got up, I found a big sack
And threw all of the hats in the bin out the back.

My feet and my knees were feeling so good
That I danced down the road for a walk in the wood.
No hats to blow off or get caught in the trees;
Just the sun on my face and my hair in the breeze.

So don't give me hats. Though you say I should wear them,
They just weigh me down and, these days, I can't bear them!

(Except for just one to keep off the sun.)

Song of life

Inspired by 'Forgiveness' by Jacob Groth, theme song of the TV series *The Eagle*

I am the spirit of life.
I travel through time
On an endless journey.

I am born of the Sun,
The earth and the air,
And the endless ocean.

I am the sower of seeds,
The reaper of crops,
In an endless harvest.

I sing for each birth,
And mourn for each death
In an endless anthem.

I am the sculptor of worlds,
The painter of light
On an endless canvas.

I weave the threads of the past
In the web of today
And an endless future.

I bind the pages of time
And the life of the Earth
In an endless circle.

Storms

Blow, winds of change,
   and take me where you will.
I will ride the raging storm
   and revel in my going.
I am a frail ship,
   Adrift on an angry sea,
And the song of the tempest
   is all around me.

But there is a place for me
   in a faraway land,
And there will be peace for me there,
   when the storm dies
And the winds give birth
   to the whisper of spring.

And I am going there
   to lift my face to the sun;
To teach my silent, sorrowing heart
   once more to sing.

Now, for the first time

I have been condemned by only one in all the Earth.
Only you and you alone denied my worth,
And in your hurt and anger could you see
That you condemned yourself to pain along with me?
That bleak loneliness of being loved with words of hate,
And hated with words that mock our onetime love,
Of seeing only others receive the gentleness of strength
And the laughter that heals all sorrows;
Could it truly end, finish, and be gone forever?
Could the woman you condemned become again a bride?
Could she know the man you are for others
Without the pain of accusation
Bringing winter's cold tears of anger deep inside?

Sometimes sunlight and laughter have danced before me
Like sunbeams in a waterfall.
In joy I reached out, touched them, and found them gone
Like leaves on the autumn wind.
Sometimes I saw a shadow, fleeting, mysterious and beautiful,
An image of gentle love.
In joy I followed, dancing, seeking,
Longing for something I never seemed to find.

Now, for the first time, I leave to go away,
Feeling it could be beautiful to stay.
Now, for the first time, I sense the warmth of pride
That woman should have to be man's bride.
Is it possible to love him – he who condemned –
And yet be free?
And if I trusted you – now, for the first time –
Would you cherish me?

Lavender

Lavender from yesterday

A little bunch of lavender, dry now
With only the faintest hint of times gone by;
It's such a small souvenir of past loveliness,
Its ribbon faded and crushed.
But the joy it recalls echoes long down the years.

Lavender for today

Her scented purple petticoats aflutter,
She stands, face to the sun.
Drifting fragrance stops the weary traveller
For a moment of memory and joy.
Aaaaaah… Lavender!

Candlelight

Why hide from me, my love?
Don't blow out the candle.
You are beautiful.
I want to love you with my eyes.
Summer has turned you to gold.
Your skin is velvet smooth.
The candlelight dances
On curves of light and shadow
And shining golden hair.

You are like the finest sculpture,
A Greek statue come to life
With warmth and colour,
Silky sleekness,
And firm, beautiful curves.

If you smile at me now,
My breath catches in my throat.
My hands follow my eyes
As if my whole awareness
Lies in those firm-smooth
Curves of your body.

A flame too hot within.
Too much. I shut my eyes
And bury my face in your hair.
Your fragrance fills my being.
I feel with my whole body
That golden touch of your skin.

End our loneliness, my love.
Hold me. Make me a part
Of your beautiful body
And feel the beating of my heart.

Love is a flower

Inspired by the song 'The Rose'

Love is a flower.
This you have told me.
This you have given me
In the words of a song.
Yes, love is a flower, beloved.
You have shown me truly.
I hold a rose for you in my thoughts
When the night is long.

Love is a flower.
It gains strength from the sunshine
   Of smiles and laughter,
And also from the raindrops
   Of tears and pain.
In winter you may not see it
   Beneath the cold snows of loneliness,
But in the spring when the sun melts the snows
   The warmth of joy will bring it forth again.

Little girl – little flower

Little flower, reach upwards
And smile at the sun above.
Laugh with us in innocence,
And trust us with your love.
There may be clouds, dark days,
And rain to make you grow.
There will be voices, winding ways,
Too many things to know.
But you will grow strongly.
You will be filled with pride.
Your heart is full of sunshine
No clouds will ever hide.
Growing brings tears as well as joy,
But one day when you are grown,
There will be happiness in tending
A little flower of your own.

Dawn of womanhood

You are a rose, sweet friend,
A rose with crimson, dewy petals,
Opening your heart to Life's harsh, careless touch.
You stand, trembling, in the mists of your early morning,
Fearful of Freedom's bright daylight,
Afraid of the wide landscape of solitude,
And the biting cold of loneliness and pain.
Tenderly you wait for love to warm you.
You know him not.
You wait in eagerness, and yet in fear,
For already you know his selfish shadow
Whose cold touch has chilled you with a pale mockery of love.
Imagine, sweet rose, how golden and how filled with joy
How warm, how beautiful that new sunlight.
A whole world will be yours in which to sing and dance.
A whole world will be yours to fill with your delight.
And you are surely chosen for your beauty.
Love picks you especially for his bride.
The wind will not scatter your petals,
Or the frosts of pain wither you on your stem.
You will not lie beneath the feet of other heedless lovers,
Trampled. You are too lovely.
Many will know the perfume of your sweetness,
And you will be a song of joy forever in the heart of Love.
And it is certain. Your day is dawning.
Nothing can stop your sunrise
Or turn your tide.
Turn your face to the sun, sweet rose,
And open wide.

Love letters

Speak love to me, my dearest.
The language of love is a caress.
You may be a thousand miles away
And yet you touch me still
If you call me 'My Love'.
Your words of love are like a hymn.
To hear them is like living in a song.
Words of love are like the gentle touch
That tames wild horses, or the embrace
That comforts loneliness of spirit.
Words of love speak straight from one heart to another
With only moonbeams in between.
Your thoughts are closed to me,
And that is only right,
For your thoughts are yours alone.
But in the words of love you share with me
My image sitting in your heart.
And I can live within the thoughts
You choose to show me;
And together in love we lie
Even when apart.

The sun in your hair

I have a well of laughter,
A warmth like summer fire,
Bright as the sun through half-shut eyes,
And the rich black velvet of desire.

Do you remember, Lover,
A walk in the wind by the sea?
The beach was deserted and we were alone
With the seagulls flying free.

We laughed and we touched
And our footprints met,
And washed from the sand
Where the sand was wet.
The wind was warm
And the summer heat
Was a fire in the dry sand
That burned our feet.
So we laughed and we danced
And ran up to the dunes
To lie in the grasses
Where the whispering tunes
Of the sea-wind sighed
Over moving sands.
Then we were naked
And the touch of your hands
Caressed my breasts
As you kissed my lips,
And moved your hands down
To the curve of my hips.

Through half-shut eyes
I saw you kneeling,
The sun in your hair
And the seagulls wheeling
Above.
   Oh Lover, how beautiful!

Then you bent down to me
And I rose up to you;
Your kisses were searching
For the secrets you knew
In the flower of my loving
Open and needing.
The world disappeared;
I was lost and unheeding
Of all but the stars
In my black velvet night.
The whole world was gone
In a shower of delight.
   Oh Lover, how beautiful!

Then you came to me, took me
In the last of my fire,
And I felt your warm firmness
The strength of desire.
I held you in love
And I loved you in laughter,
And we lay on the sand
In the warm sun after.

Now I have a well of laughter,
And a memory of summer fire,
Bright as the sun through half-shut eyes,
And the rich black velvet of desire.

You touched my day

When I awoke that morning – yesterday,
I stood in the morning light and breathed the sunrise air,
My heart beating like the wings of a bird,
Awake to all of life before me there.
It was a day of destiny, of mingled joy and sorrow,
And it took me through the rich red of passion
To peace like a sky of blue,
And you, my friend, touched my day of destiny
With an extra depth of feeling.
I will remember you.

Perfection at sunset

Moisture beads on the round belly of the glass
As I hold it up to the slanting light of the sinking sun.
Water droplets scatter the light into a thousand tiny rainbows.
The wine is pale translucent gold with a hint of green.
The aroma speaks of fruit, new-mown grass, and lemons.
Cool droplets run from the glass as I tilt it to my lips
And the burst of flavour sits like rainbows on my tongue.
This is the very essence of late summer and the fruits of the season.
Ah…Verdelho!

Christmas dinner was scrumptious

Christmas dinner smelled scrumptious. The tree sparkled bright.
Young Jeremy's eyes were alive with delight.
He'd wakened at dawn to this wonderful day.
His presents were opened, the toys spread for play.

He'd driven his toy cars around for a while,
And heaped up the wrappings in a colourful pile.
Now he was hungry, and bored with the waiting
Surely his sister had done decorating
How long could it take to prepare a Pavlova,
With luscious whipped cream and berries all over?

He could hear lots of giggles, out there in the kitchen.
If a bowl needed scraping, perhaps he could pitch in.
And when would the turkey be brought out to eat?
His tummy was begging at the smell of roast meat.
'When's dinner?' he called, climbing up on his chair.
'Now!' said his sister, bringing gravy with care.

She and his dad sat down in their seats
And made room on the cloth for all of the eats.
Mum came to the door, a big plate in each hand,
But alas! The grand entry did not go as planned
Dad sat with the carvers. He was all already
But champagne in the kitchen had made Mum unsteady.
Forward she stepped onto Jeremy's cars
And down she went heavily, tits over arse

The roast and pavlova flew high through the air
And the pav flopped down, smack, onto Jeremy's hair
In horrified silence everyone froze
As berries and cream ran right down his nose
Jeremy stuck out his tongue with a flick
And gave all that ooze a bit of a lick
Soon he was licking as fast as he could
'Mmm! Dinner is scrumptious. It's ever so good!'

Woman with flowers

You met a woman,
A woman with flowers,
And you stepped through her doorway
For just a few hours.

And she was the laughter
Of friendship's delight,
And barefoot she walked
On the grass of your night.

And she taught you a secret
That nobody knows –
If your heart yearns for freedom
Just smile at a rose.

The desert wind

The wind from the north-west breathed fire as it came
From the heart of the desert, and whispered your name
In my ear as I stirred in the night, and I dreamed
Of the touch of your hands and your kiss, and it seemed
Once again we made love and were joined in the night,
In discovery, in need, and in laughing delight,
Your body in mine – the sweet taste of your mouth;
And I sent you my kiss on the wind from the south.

Reconciling

I saw you standing there in the last rays of the daylight,
With your eyes half shut, searching the light of the setting sun
For the face you knew. And my heart leapt within me,
And all of my senses rose – intensified,
And the evening breeze became already
A forecast of your hands toughing my face and hair.

I hardly noticed the walking to you.
My eyes were intently on your face.
Was there a crowd around us?
I cannot remember. I saw only you.
The touch of your hand brought a fire that burned me,
The nearness of you like a whirlpool drawing me in;
And you took me into your arms and held me,
Crying with joy – melting like snow in the sun.

Later, we stripped away the veils of pain and distance
Until we were naked in spirit as in flesh.
I showed you my sorrow for the pain between us,
Seeking to heal it by giving you the feelings in my heart.
I caressed your skin and hair, and kissed you,
Needing to be close again to all I loved.

Then we were joined once more in love and joy.
I felt as though I were falling,
Falling through an eternity of darkness filled with brilliant stars.
Just as ever happened for us, for a moment time stood still.
Love had triumphed – had conquered pain, anger and sorrow.
Oh tell me it can, sweet lover. Tell me it always will.

Tears and ecstasy

Love light, shine on me.
Fill my soul with ecstasy.
With your gifts I'm overflowing.
Oh the sweetest pain of knowing
All the joy of life's fulfilment
In a single precious moment.

Take me not back into darkness.
Let me live within your brightness.
Hear my song of liberation,
Song of hope, Love's incantation,
Hymn of joy to you ascending,
Prayer for freedom never ending.

Love light, guide my living.
Fill me with the power of giving.
Let me see your face more clearly.
Let me walk with you more nearly.
Guide me through my human sorrow
To the sunshine of tomorrow.

See me now before you kneeling,
Filled with such a depth of feeling,
Filled at last with realisation
Of the pain of human failing.
Touch my heart and come to me.
Change my tears to ecstasy.

The anchor and the wind

When you build your house and plant your garden,
You put an anchor-stone forever on your life,
And yet it is a work of love, a warm belonging,
To give your freedom gladly to your wife.

Then children born of love are gladly welcomed,
The love you give returned a thousand-fold,
But they will bind you close for half a lifetime;
Your freedom serves their needs as you grow old.

And yet there is a part of you that knows no bondage,
That roams through other lives and other worlds,
That knows the songs of solitude, of wind and water,
And all the pain and joy a heart can hold.

You take these images of life and songs of feeling –
You take them in secret back to your family and your home,
Your house of memories. The walls whisper in silence
Of other realities, solitude, and space to roam.

I know the man who lived beyond your garden.
He touched me slowly, gently, as a misty dawn.
Our solitudes were shared with laughter and roses.
Our moments of time are past, but never gone.

A better life

Perhaps it is a better life
To be a 'friend' and not a wife.
A 'friend' can have romance and fun,
And independence, all in one;
And if he tells her what to do,
She doesn't have to follow through.
She can say 'Yes' if opportunity knocks,
And doesn't have to wash his socks!

Images of love

Love can flow like the tide,
With as many forms as clouds on an autumn day.
It can be as brilliant as sunset over the ocean,
Or burn like dry sand in the summer sun.
It can whisper like the voice of ages in a sea shell,
And caresses like moonlight on a midsummer sea.

Love can be cruel as a winter storm,
Crying with the voice of gulls riding the gale,
As harsh as the grey surf pounding a deserted shore
When sea and sky are indistinguishable.

But real love is never vile or repulsive.
It is a gift to be cherished, however it is given.
Without love, our lives would lack dimension.
To give love, and to receive, together make us whole.

No gift of love

No gift of love, friendship or sharing
Is lost, wasted or wrong,
However insignificant or strange it be,
However brief the moment or however long.

To touch another with thoughts of friendship
Is beautiful.
But I will not try to make my friend belong.
I cannot buy his soul, or own his solitude,
And seeking to limit his world to fit my own
Is always wrong.

The prophets

Inspired by Leonard Cohen's 'Suzanne'

Once I met a prophet who walked beside a river.
He saw the water flowing from the past into the future.
When he spoke they listened, but the rulers could not hear him.
They were deaf to earthly visions, blind to words of wisdom,
Looking only to each other and to gold for signs of wonder,
So his words passed by like shadows, or the sound of distant thunder.

I want to hear his wisdom. I want to see his vision.
Lift me up to see above the temples of the cities,
To hear beyond the chatter of the crowds of nameless voices,
To feel beyond the pain of their crushed and failing choices

Long ago another prophet walked out into the desert,
He let life's rage and turmoil flow out into the wasteland,
Where the sands around him sang of water lost forever.
As his arms reached up for mercy to the vultures high above him,
The sunlight flowed upon him and filled him like a river.
Enough for many lifetimes, so he became a giver.

I want to hear his wisdom. I want to see his vision.
Lift me up to see above the temples of the cities,
To hear beyond the chatter of the crowds of nameless voices,
To feel beyond the pain of their crushed and failing choices

We take the gifts of prophets but cannot comprehend them,
Pretending understanding but believing we know better.
We pin them to our lives as pretty decorations,
But cannot make a place for them in times of building nations.
Let me hear those many voices of warning, loss and pain
But also listen truly for how to hope again.

I want to hear their wisdom. I want to see their vision.
Lift me up to see above the temples of the cities,
To hear beyond the chatter of the crowds of nameless voices,
To feel beyond the pain of our crushed and failing choices.

Why?

Why would you make of love a chain
To shackle your heart and mind?
Why would you choose to live in pain –
Your freedom so to bind?

Why would you make of your thoughts a cage,
And clip the wings of love?
Love is an eagle who should fly free
In the sun in the sky above.

Why would you limit the range of your joy?
Give it the whole of the Earth.
Each moment is special. Each evening is peace,
Each morning a fresh new birth.

Reconciliation: Returning

Are you the wild west wind
Or the springtime willow?
Am I the iron butterfly
Or a flower of the meadow?

For you, perhaps, I might laugh and smile
And flourish in the sun.
For me, perhaps, you might bend and yet be strong,
That, separately, our lives might yet be one.

Te Wai-Iti morning

In the first light of that last beautiful morning,
I awoke and watched your sleeping face.
The room was full of the pale light of sunrise.
Your eyes were closed. Your face was filled with peace.
Love rose like a wave on the sea within me.
Truly, to watch you unobserved delights my eye.
And filled with happiness I went to the window
To part the curtains and look up at the morning sky.

   Bird song at dawning,
        Rising sun in the mist over sapphire lake,
   Blue-green hills in the morning,
        And joy of love – a memory to make.

I walked softly through the doorway
Out into the fresh, cool morning air,
And stood for a long time on your balcony,
Alive to all the peace and beauty there.
Then I walked once more down across the lawn.
The grass was cool and damp beneath my feet.
The apple tree cast a long shadow in the pink light of dawn.
Never had I tasted apples quite so sweet.
I reached up to gently touch an apple
They were all the sweeter when you placed them in my hand.
Then I turned and came inside to wake you,
And we loved once more before I left your land.

Often my thoughts fly back to Te Wai-Iti,
Into the sunrise, far across the sea.
My heart still walks in the mists of your distant garden,
And my love hangs still like an apple on your tree.
And I am still surprised by the beauty of our sharing,
And the warmth of love and joy you gave to me.

Reflection

When you look into my eyes
Can you see your reflection,
Your image looking back?
And can you recognise yourself
In mirror image?

Look closely.
My eyes will tell you something
A mirror cannot tell,
For in my eyes
You are all of my desires,
My happiness, my wellspring of content.
You are the most special person
My eyes have ever seen.
In my eyes you stand alone, my love,
Where no other has ever been.

For a troubled woman friend

My dearest friend, I do declare,
You're negatively self-aware,
'Intolerant', a 'shitty cook',
'Guilty', 'sick', with filthy look!
You tell me you've been getting pissed.
You even hate your analyst.
By all the saints (and WERE they males??),
Your life is going off the rails.
Well, dear friend, I've news for you.
I know exactly what to do.
Go straight down to the church and pray
To God – She'll take your woes away.
She made me what I truly am,
A source of puzzlement to man,
A bitch who laughs behind her hand,
Whose soul belongs in 'no-man's-land'.
Show me a man. We'll make out fine,
But he will find my soul is MINE.
Am I sorry? No I'm not.
I'm laughing now at what I've got.
Life is a ball. Come dance with me.
You are WOMAN. You are FREE.

Sonnet – What chance of eco-harmony?

We spread our crystal traps to catch the sun,
Our tanks and dams to hold the fickle rain
We cared for parks and forests every one
And sought to halt pollution's ugly gain.

Industrialists and businessmen now spoke
Of many jobs, of wealth, the modern mine
Of export markets, services bespoke
And automating businesses online.

But can these two views merge to give us one?
Can calls for smaller impacts meet desire
For larger industries, more riches won,
And market growth to take our income higher?

It seems at first too great a gap to cover
Unless we truly can care for each other.

Why does my heart sing?

Why does my heart sing
With the nearness of you,
Almost as though your presence
Spoke the music of love into my heart?

Why does my body tremble
In response to your lightest touch,
Almost as though your hand were the wind
Setting the leaves of my tree a-dancing?

Why do your eyes meeting mine
Light such a fire within,
Almost as though my heart were aflame,
Leaping upwards into the sun?

Such a long, short time it is
Since that first night you held me close to your heart,
And our own special miracle is a love that grows
Ever more warm and beautiful from that magic start.

Pain

When it is night the distances are greater, the pain is deeper,
And the heart feels more alone.
If it were possible I would bring you the one you love,
Even if only for tonight.
Love and sorrow have walked hand-in-hand for you.
Tonight you walk with sorrow, in the shadow of love,
And my heart mourns for your burning tears.

Would that I could be with you this night, my friend.
Not to make love as lovers do,
But sometimes even a wrong presence is better than emptiness,
The loneliness not so finally alone.
I would be a pillow for your weeping,
I would hear your pain, and taste the salt of your tears.
And even if the night were long,
Still would I stay with you until the need was gone.
Words need not pass between us
But I would wrap my arms around you
And lay my face against your hair.
If it were possible, my friend,
I would wish the touch of my hands upon you
Might ease your sorrow,
Even if only for one night.

If it were possible, as little children believe,
To end pain with a kiss,
Then I would give you such a kiss,
And steal from you your pain.
Gladly would I bear it for you,
This night, until the end of need.
Without words I would tell you –
Tell you with this self-same kiss –
To have loved thus deeply is the discovery of the soul.
If love should die, discovery lives on,
A half-joy deep in the heart.
Poor will he be who never finds it.
Rich will you be, even in sorrow.

Who are you?

Who are you, my friend?
Why do you have such a restless spirit?
I open my soul to you,
But when I look into your eyes
You look away.

Why do you hide from friends
Who reach out to gently touch you?
There are many who love you deeply,
But still your spirit prowls the night –
Calling.

What do you need of life and those who love you
That you should come home to rest?
Do you know?
Are you afraid to tell us who you are,
Even knowing that we love you?
Or is it us who fail to hear you?

The Other Woman

What can I give you, my sister,
To show that I mean you no harm?
If I stood before you
I would be shy,
But filled with respect.
Will you take from me a smile?
My friendship?
A flower from my garden?
A kiss? Perhaps even my tears?

I cannot give you back your man,
For he has never left you,
In spirit or in fact.
In my presence
He thinks of you always.
Already you have my gifts,
Although you may not know it,
For what I have given him of myself
He has brought to you with is love.

Just for one moment
How beautiful it would be
To complete the circle –
To touch your hand.

There was a man

There was a man who reached out to touch my world.
Gently he held it, like some precious butterfly
Plucked and set free from the depths of a spider's web.
There was a man whose memory is written in my heart,
For he gave it the sunlight of rich fulfilment,
And the rain of knowing the sweet pain of ecstasy.
And I opened for him, unfolding
Like a rose blooming for the first time in his garden.
There was a man who made me tremble with my need for him,
His touch upon my body like a flame kindling desire.
For him I swept away the outer layers of my loving
And showed him my passion to its burning core.
When he came to me, I met him in joy with kisses,
My heart beating like the wings of a bird within.
We did not need disguises, or the clothes of our daily living.
Together, our nakedness became perfection.
Were we not born this way? Were we not meant to come together?
And my hands sought to know all of him, and then my kisses,
For he was the alter of my offering to love, and I was his;
And he knew me in all the depths of my body,
The darkness, the desire, the warmth of my inner night.
We were gentleness. We were strength.
We were storms on the seas of the earth,
And the winds of heaven bearing each other
From the cliff's edge into the sky,
Joined together into one perfect body, suspended
For all eternity in a fragment of time.

And we were the calm after the storm,
The gentle warmth of the sun after rain.
Even in sleep, I felt joined with him
By a sense of warm belonging.
Even when parted we remained
In some way two halves of one whole,
Now my world still bears the imprint of his hand,
And his memory lives still within my heart.

When I was lost

When I was lost,
    It was you who found me.
When the sun would not shine for me,
    You gave me your smile.
When the night was lonely,
    You brought me friendship.
When I was weak,
    You taught me strength.
When I was hurting,
    You gave me comfort.
When I was troubled,
    You sent me peace.
When I was unworthy,
    You gave me my pride.

And, oh, the precious joy of knowing
That just for myself – you gave me your love.

After the storm

It takes time
After the storm
For clouds to clear and distant thunder to fade,
For the sun to warm the earth and dry the leaves,
For flowers to open and life to begin again.

It takes time
After the storm
Time for the grass to grow
Where floods scarred the earth
And the river changed its course.

It takes time
After the storm
For the fallen trees to be shrouded,
Covered in new growth
And, in a new way, to belong.

It takes time
After the storm
For the new to become the accepted,
Time to recall the way things were without regret
And walk into the future with a newfound sense of hope.

Pity the troubadour

A short play in verse for light entertainment

Narrator: Let's take an imaginative trip back in time to the dark ages – to a world of knights, damsels, and daring deeds – a time when the Scots and English fought each other across the border and cattle thieves were local heroes.

In those days of castles and manor houses, home entertainment was nothing like what we have today. Just think about it – there were no movies, no TV, no recorded music, and the only book around (even supposing anyone in the household could read) was the Holy Bible.

You can well imagine that folks might have got a bit tired of entertaining themselves with the Laird's tales of the past battles and deer hunts, Cousin Ewan's lute, and Young Frederick's love songs. The visit of a travelling troubadour to sing new songs and tell new tales would have been an exciting novelty.

(*Waves the troubadour forward to the stage*) But you have to feel a little pity for the troubadour. He was expected to provide entertainment across the board for young and old, drunk or sober – gentle young ladies, callow lads, battle-hardened knights, and raucous, bawdy serving wenches. By just looking around a hall filled with people, it must have been hard to judge each new audience and pitch the presentation right.

Troubadour: Indeed so! I'm having that same trouble here today looking around at you all. However, I'm going to assume you're gentlefolk, and tell you a tale of the notorious highlander, McTavish. (*Recites the following tale*)

He entered the room with a crash of the door
And a clatter of spurs on the stones of the floor
His cloak swirled around him, snowflakes blew past
The watchers reeled back with the shock of the blast.

'Where is McTavish, that villain so low?
He rode out this way, so where did he go?
I swear by my sword he will die now, today
And if you're protecting him, you too will pay.'

The watchers sat silent in shock as he paced
Slashing the air with his sword as he faced
The lords at their table, dogs at their feet
With a feast set in front of them ready to eat.

Lady Ellen stood up from her stool by the fire.
Unhurried came she to face the knight's ire.
Good sir, I can help you. Pray sheathe your sword
I know where McTavish bides. You have my word.

Yes, he came past, yesterday at sunrise
I was walking the dogs with the keep yet to rise.
He asked for the speediest way to Glen Morris
So I showed him the north way that leads through the forest.

He tarried no more, but rode off with his men
Soon out of my sight and not seen again.
If you seek him you'll need to ride north with all haste
He's a full day ahead – not a second to waste.

The knight whirled around and strode to the door
It crashed shut behind him. The wind ceased to roar.
Snow flurries settled and melted in silence.
A thudding of hooves faded into the distance.

The dogs now relaxed and their hackles went down.
Lady Ellen stood tall in her wimple and gown.
'God's teeth,' said the Laird. 'Woman, what have you done?
You know that McTavish is one of our own.

You've betrayed him no less. How could you do it!
I swear if he dies, by God's oath you'll rue it.'
'Fear not, my Lord,' Lady Ellen replied.
'McTavish lives yet, and is right at my side.'

At her words an old woman, hooded in brown
Stood up near the fire and uncloaked her gown.
'McTavish!' the Laird cried out in surprise.
'How well you have hidden yourself in this guise.'

McTavish bowed low. 'I had fair Ellen's aid.
She is clever and lovely, and never afraid.
If she will have me, I seek her to wife.
I would give her my loyalty my love and my life.'

Raising her hand to his lips he knelt down
Then bending, he kissed the hem of her gown.
As he rose to his feet the Laird laughed with delight.
'God's teeth, man, this is indeed a strange night.

Of course if she wishes, you both have my blessing.
That's a fine reason now to get back to our feasting.
McTavish, for someone who could have been dead,
You've done very well to come out of it wed!'

The watchers all cheered, and ale flowed like water
And that's how McTavish won the Laird's lovely daughter.

Audience 'plants': Boo! Hiss! Too tame! Tell us what really happened!

Troubadour: Oh, so you're not quite the gentlefolk I took you for. All right, all right! Settle down! Here's what really happened. (*Recites the following*)

He entered the room with a crash of the door
And a clatter of spurs on the stones of the floor.
His cloak swirled around him, snowflakes blew past.
The Laird's guests reeled back with the shock of the blast.

Six Englishmen followed, filling the hall.
Frightening and fierce-looking giants were they all.
Shields held in front of them, swords poised for evil,
They snarled at the watchers like spawn of the devil

The Laird then stood up from his place at the table.
'What do you want? We'll do as we're able.'
'I believe,' roared the knight, 'you have stolen my cattle.
My best cow alone is well worth a battle.

Tell me this instant where they've been taken,
Or sorry you'll be, if I'm not mistaken.'
'Sir Knight,' said the Laird, 'we know not of your cattle.
Surely you haven't been listening to prattle.'

But the knight just declared with a thunderous brow,
'A curse on your castle, I demand my prize cow!'
Well, there in the firelight, her loveliness clear,
Sat young Lady Ellen, quaking in fear.

The knight crossed the room to the stool where she sat,
Threw her up onto his shoulder and spat
At the feet of her father, the laird, as he said,
'She'll be my prize. If you thwart me you're dead.

I'll take her right now. I'm ready and able.'
So saying, he flung her across the main table
With a scattering of goblets and plates falling down
And with one hand he ripped the front from her gown.

The watchers all gasped at such beauty laid bare.
Even the knight could do naught but stare.
Now her wimple fell off, and her gold hair fell clear
And she cursed her foul captor, in spite of her fear.

While the knight was distracted came a move at the door.
In strode McTavish with a furious roar.
Dirk in his hand, he leapt on the knight.
'You thought you'd take her, but I'll take you tonight'

So saying he slashed the knight's throat side-to-side.
He fell and the red blood flowed free as he died.
His six men now leaderless made for the doorway
But the Laird's men leapt up and spitted them anyway.

'Enough' cried the Laird. 'We're all done and dusted.
Thanks to McTavish this raid is now busted.
Clean up the blood, toss the dead out the door.
It's time to get back to feasting some more.'

McTavish helped fair lady Ellen to stand.
He gave her his cloak; she gave him her hand.
'Kind sir, I owe you my maidenhead, pure.
I'm yours if you'll have me, of that I am sure.'

McTavish bowed low and kissed her fair hand.
'My lady, of all the young maids in this land
You are the one I would choose for my wife.
I pledge you my loyalty, my love and my life.'

'Where is the priest? Let us quickly be wed.
Our "feasting" tonight can be in my bed!'
Father Buchanan stood up and came over
As everyone cheered the brave maid and her lover.

Linking their hands, he heard their vows said
Then as they knelt he declared they were wed.
The Laird rose to toast them and laughed with delight.
'God's teeth, man, this is indeed a strange night.

Ellen, my dear, for a maid nearly ravished
It's lucky you are to be wed to McTavish.
And McTavish, for someone who could have been dead
You've done very well to come out of it wed!'

Everyone cheered, and the ale flowed like water
And that's how McTavish won the Laird's lovely daughter.

Troubadour: (*Bows, kisses his hand to applause, and exits the stage*)

www.ingramcontent.com/pod-product-compliance
Lightning Source LLC
Chambersburg PA
CBHW070938080526
44589CB00013B/1553